THE BALCONY TREE

Also by Christopher Middleton
from Carcanet

The Pursuit of the Kingfisher
(essays)
Two Horse Wagon Going By
Selected Writings

CHRISTOPHER MIDDLETON

The Balcony Tree

CARCANET

Acknowledgements

Grateful acknowledgement is made to the editors of *Frames, Hanging Loose, The Lace Neck Review, Ninth Decade, Numbers, Ō-Blēk, PN Review, Shearsman* and *The Threepenny Review*, in which some of these poems and prose pieces first appeared.

First published in 1992 by
Carcanet Press Limited
208-212 Corn Exchange Buildings
Manchester M4 3BQ

A CIP catalogue record for this book is
available from the British Library.
ISBN 0 85635 981 5

The publisher acknowledges financial assistance
from the Arts Council of Great Britain

Set in 10pt Garamond Simoncini by Bryan Williamson, Darwen
Printed and bound in England by SRP Ltd, Exeter

Contents

1

An Ideologist

for David Edwards

Nebulous, fractured, not too fast,
How come this ring of hair
Falls to the white I doodle on.

If I turn it around by thought
I face unfeatured distance;
It hangs in the moon for luck.

Masts that were trees creak,
With cobalt sky bamboo combines,
And spiteful critics rule the roost:

Spirit is fierce, it contradicts,
Only a presuming, only a wizened
Spirit carps and backbites.

Attend. Soon my bamboo palace
Bathes in the pool that winked
From the fracture of that iron hair.

Unshod I see the earth, old nag,
Shake off its flies and epithets
And run like a cloud with the moon.

Ancient Lace

Sitting silent and a long time gone
Hearing the tower clock strike faraway two
Feeling the sun toil in the skin of your face
Truth to tell waiting ain't so bad he said
Listen to the Carolina wren

Try not to let things ever get you down he said
Carolling like she found a roach to eat
Zucchini zucchini she call in the green bamboo
Tower clock won't ever strike a two the same he said
That's Emmy now knocking on a wood block

Or it's a kitchen pot she could be knocking on
The little changes bring you back to earth he said
No great shakes plain poor old earth he said
But now by heaven that was a woodpecker
Real weird it snickers with a hiccup

Don't always put your life on the line he said
A great shit heap out there and me and you
Leastways we settle up to be a whiff of it
Ten feet up today looking across the town
What speaks to you makes all the difference he said

Might be that little stick of frankincense you lit
Burning in the tree tub and a Carolina wren
And a stroke or two on a bell and a bird's note
It's good when things pierce your heart a moment
Make it pure he said and plenty more than heaven did

It's that warm the sun to melt your mask he said
And did they bring any wine for them to sip
So be it if they did not and enough's enough
Long time since like shooting stars they did set off
Suppose their whispering brocades will pass this way

Anguish

Suppose he stays out in the cold
With towers around him floodlit
And the big birds that shriek around the towers in a trio
And around the birds the sky
Silent as the tomb at two in the morning

This time he can't come back
Often before, he might drift back in, not only for his coat
Paradise was near enough in his belief
He only had to march around himself indoors
To the flick of my eyelids
Making the dreams of men tormented come true

For certain he'll be back, dripping wet
A mess, river weed stuck to his ribs, clammy
And a cold story to tell the children
How he peered up the birds' backsides
Put his arms in the warm sleeves of their wings
Flew first around the towers, then on to paradise

An Angel

Old men who beat their wives
Magyars with feet of mahogany
Mexicans with hearts of gold
They pin me to the wall
And ask for admissions

But young men and women too
Stand sick in a crooked line
Crazies gone to the clinic
Eyeballs falling out
Ask for my admissions

Scholars crouch in a line
Pointing at me rifles
Do I have their secret?
Butchers form a line with cleavers
Lung of pork and sawdust jawbone

– Of my slaughterhouse
The double doors on them I shut
Let them eat some other eyeballs
Let them eat their tripod noses
Altogether somewhere else

Me I frisk
In a fastness of dew
Highly microscopic
I will eat their bullets
Nor drop my positive disguises

Old shop fusty as hawkflight hide me
Implements of domestic torture
Hide me for the wink of a lifetime
Hide me drums that tumbled
When bit by bit a temple exploded

Folks I only ask you hide me
Sickening butchers look for me
And silken scholars think otherwise
Crooked as they come withal
But hoping somewhat

Then from a blackened book
Letters wrought of rock and water
Composing the raven's flight in chipped flint
Quitting my volcano
The devil I skip and frisk for thee

Bird Watching

Old folks with big faces
Get off their big butts
And raise binoculars

Roving for miles and floated so
Open-eyed by their thermals
They come to watch us birds

Finding in fresh air a life style
They are intrigued by blue bunting
To the loon's cry their red hearts caracol

For them we save the day with our tricks
Quaint compulsive ceremonies we perform
Delight back to life in them a long disbanded soul

Rare though they breathe down our necks
We can peck at hickory to suit their book
But when they learn, when they learn to call

Call and be recognized flamingo lakes
Will be for their pink flocks the habitat
They will squat and blink to be owl

Slowly their web of being will float out
Never to hold for long if at all
The thing they never knew how to desire

One day they will know one another
In several ways they once ignored
Nesting in dells and rocks they drove us from

One day ruffling our big butts and faces
We too will ask what secret glory possessed them
We too will watch and want it all

Still Small Voice

When you come to my country, tell me
Why was it, why did you travel so far
What you know of the place you are from, tell me
Fear not the place where you are

Tell me what you heard, many sounds, one by one
Tell me the rain, a dog's howl, out in the dark
Rustle of the dust under a footsole
Tell me a spoon, a dish, a dish, a spoon

The pooled light spread in a vine of colours
Carves through feeling roads to somewhere too
And wild saloons, a dark stream, a field with horses
A garden plot you planted six wild strawberries in, long ago
Rivers of grief that roll through flesh and time
Red holes in the ground where people weep and pray
Tell me those, if you can, I will hear them call
Where you are is half the way

When ghosts rise up, and mists, and silvery presences
You feel a quicker beat of wings in every breath of air
When the hollows open, night begins –
Or sun will spread its peacock fan, moon make hay of everything
Baskets prettily woven
People at the doors, talking, tell me
Words they speak or cannot, tunes they sing to, even
How they resist, the people, when times are hard and they can take no more

How they ache, heartbreak has to come
And how it is to be not dead, tell me the animal touch
Of a summer dawn, feathery owl's cry
Tell me the wind and walls it clings against
The stones and the water, speechless, and the skin
On everything, cherries and moles and wings
Mountain peak and egg
And what is going on, the reasoned beings being born
The wine glass cool to touch, tang of salt, canvas of a shoe
A broken ship hiding still in a skin of trees –

Braiding the split fibres of time
A shiver of desire to shape a storied music into things
Yes, and the sea to be with you, forsaken sea
Tell me the lost voices of the sea

When you come from your far land, tell me
Tell me what the changes are, their night, their day
And how it is to have believed them, tell me now:
Where you are is half the way   .

(To the tune of Pat Metheny's 'If I Could', and for Doña Brown)

Devil Lyric

Love becomes a heavy cargo
Burst loose from its ropes
In the hold it looked so harmless
Birds in cages, coffee

Now the ship rolls
The belovèd turns her face
Hundredfold as the wind
The cargo gongs around

Not so natural death
Masts rake the deep
Gulls forget the keel
Nothing to drink or nibble

The coffee and the birds
Squirm against the underdeck
Soon a dizzy squid
Has fixed them with its ink

Meanwhile drink your chicken
Carve apart your coffee
Contemplate a third
Source of some disorder

Souls that colonize
This pinball of a planet
Gulfs of glory think you
Sphincters of His Image

Michèle's Rooms

The handle of the willow basket curving
The red tiled unlevel trodden floor
At knee height the clock face but no clock body
Toy clock hands constant at twenty to six

The wooden bowl empty of apples
Balls and hanks of wool in the willow basket
The procession of sea urchin shells on the mantelpiece
The angled needles as they pierce the wool

In coloured sleeves the shelved LPs
Loops of plants I came to water
Pink of the wool and of the towering candle
Snowy bears and rabbits warm for Lola

Rising suns of scallops knitted into a shawl
The way the shawl hangs unoccupied from a hook
A mobile by the window strung with wands and ducks
The tang of wine a moment held behind the teeth

The invisibility of the hook
The absence of electricity
The plant bowl that overflowed on the telephone bill
The tiny bird crouched on the mantelpiece

The lifted latch and the opening window
The breeze that burrows through a shirt for flesh
All these marks to detect her laughter by
The word's very event in a special voice

Curve of the beak of the sacred ibis
Heart of legend locked in a nondescript replica
Spheres that only come to thought as curves completely seen
Two cracks in the wooden beam darkening them

The wooden beam's edges bevelled by an old axe
Absent from the encyclopaedia the surge of the scribe's mind
Flit of the pen's tip crossing two scraps of paper
The ghostly scribe without a name

A Revenant

Now she is here
Again, quick, in a taste
Of lemon, not even so
Much as a bite, she is here
In a whiff

Of lemon peel, no way
Even to tell
Where from, the light
Saffron perhaps, a snowy
Touch of metal

Or, afloat
On a flood of being, me,
I had drawn
A tingle out, indistinct,
A distant signal

Flashing in the hotter rush
Of air tonight, mixed
Into it, funny,
Today, the wiggle
Of a child, head back

Shrimp bodysock, she
Did a glancing
Noonday
Dance across
A crack

In a paving stone, she
Shook
At the sky
Her fist
With a flower in it

Now so long dead
Another
Is here, I remember to be
In the taste
Or touch, or in the child

A wandering
Sensation, mutely
To learn my shape, later to flit
Ghostwise from a being
I will never know

La Morena

My white cow tonight is quite silent
My white cow milking a heart from darkness

What tricks and silks will she tumble into
My white cow with opening parachute lips

My white cow with a shirt of woodsmoke
My white cow with a beehive of desires

Sometimes an abandon seizes her by the horns
Sometimes she is placid and sings in church

My white cow dancing in her field of fire
My white cow walking with dangerous steps

Everywhere she supposes there are cathedrals
Everywhere bells inscribe on air their spiral signs

My white cow with marked ideas of her own
My white cow whose tuft is a tangle of tempers

The baskets of air hang from her solid bones
The jugs of earth lift with her little breasts

My white cow who makes sorrow burn a day away
My white cow who makes sorrow bite like a shark

My white cow who shivers and penetrates men
My white cow who rides men bareback

Often conscious of too many things at one time
Often come times when she knows nothing at all

She has no clock for her timing is internal
No voice but hers alone tells her when and how

She will eat dry bread if there's none better
My white cow who tastes always of oranges

My white cow who goes one better than the snow
Her quim is heaven for whom she pleases

In the nights we stretch with furious argument
My white cow takes every word to its limit

Shortening days we walk together hand in hand
More than once she tore my arm from its socket

I will do my dance one-armed for my white cow
I love her life her ways her difficult nature

We live beneath roofs that stand centuries apart
My white cow in small towns and purple cities

My white cow in a village dances to the guitar
My white cow sipping wine from a cup of clay

When the baskets are hanging bright in the water
They fill with her fish and creak in earthquake

When in my white cow's hair old stories are told
We stop them to start the world afresh redeemed

She is absent in the canyon of her red lust
She is present in the ordinary dishes we eat off

My white cow is a black one to tell the truth
Or else Chinese or else some kind of Arabian

To call her cow at all is a profound mistake
She is a leopard with four cubs in a forest

My white cow in that hotel stripping off her clothes
My white cow who is not mine at all

My white vanishing cow with her dolphin legs
My white cow who wades *toute nue* in the Toulourenc

Her skin mirrors itself and that is it for us
I fall into her skin to oblige Lord Shock

I tongue my white cow in her purity and playfulness
She will never come around to believing I mean it

My white cow imagines me far off running away
Little does she know I run to catch her leaping form

White cow who dances wild in the middle of the world
White cow your sweet dust with the wind blowing over it

Cybele

It is cold outside so she has walked in
Loving my feet for her own good reasons,

Straight in, tail up, scanning the kitchen
She discovers nothing but a desire

So at my feet she winds and unwinds
Her calico skin. When I tap at the blotter

Up she lifts a paw, forgets, listens again,
Looking elsewhere, if elsewhere is anywhere

And curls in a fit of abandon
Around the tongue of my tennis shoe.

Her paw milks the lace, her paw milks the ankle bone,
Amorously unparticular she forgets her milk

Habit, suddenly crouches, licking her tail:
Suddenly I know nothing for her is sudden

For she forgets her forgotten tail, silent
She explores cavity, cavity, for instance

Behind the cutting block propped against
The wall, she has found a fascination

Shadow or moonlight there, scampers off
In a rage of vague desire for shadow

And foot, the raw smell of shadow and foot,
She's stepping over hollows everywhere

And finding what she wants to be hidden there,
Everything new, glistening cushion, clay

Horse, fragile, over it she has to step
A soft way. What invisible spasms of being

Span her heart beat? How come she detects
Here in this room the moon she only knows

From green by the shadows moon-eye makes
Nothing of? Smells are shape, the sharp

Outline of mouse, the cry of yucca white
She evidently smells when tasting my feet.

Not my feet. Them, me she ignores. It is
A very sweet crisis to be constantly cat:

Her senses, precise as Gieseking's fingers,
Track a music, her veins are shivering with it –

Transformation, the furnace of horror
Red in her claw, fact in her leap of fire –

She is arrow, target. The bird, a flit
She hesitates to hear, could prong her

Against a sky that is no sky for her
But promise of open, beak, edible, never

Depressive, it stings, strikes, white glistens.
Bone aches too that way in my meat.

The China Virgins

They tinkle in their glass
Voices more thin than shrill
Coils of mist they penetrate remote hill temples
They are fire tongues capping spires of thought
They inhabit oblongs of ice in orange juice

Often they appear when creation begins
In memory
They rub their fingers and glow when you lose your mule
Hungering footsore in a Tibet of aimlessness
Like an onset of birdsong in heartbreak they capture you

Cool outrush of force
In the construction of a seashell
Meandering prolonged across symmetry breaks
They delineate an evolution
They round the roof of a wren's nest

Pop of champagne cork
Snap of elastic against firm muscle
If not so then slow motioning the convolvulus display
Tremor of a voice when it has caught the drift
Of white bone powder blown across the Gobi

Breath of wind bending the crest of a catalpa
Also the clatter when catalpa bean pods fall
The sputter when wet has called for the surge
Of a body incandescent but then backs off
The china virgins recoil to advance

On the back of matter they pound their bright fists
Flash their eyes in the twice five parabolas of a Leticia's legs

A parchment swept by fingers
Sidereal coin
A nymph spinning struck into the hot silver centre
A song that drinks the scent of a space unborn
Nothing nothing but a phrase no sooner uttered
Than questioned as to its calligraphy
Nothing sooner questioned than the china virgins

Dust with Whisky

Solo the locomotive horn responding
Hollows out the heat of night,

The North American locomotive horn
Responds to the cool, peculiarly

Strained (sausage meat forsooth
Loading a tube of sheep gut)

Contralto warble of Clara Butt.
Dame Clara sings from a *tomba oscura*,

Under mortal pressure Damosel Clara sings,
So profound her breath, dense her tone

They model in air the swept cone of an old
Phonograph horn. Frilling its orifice,

Waves of tin harbour a painted rose,
And fragrant sound, purple enough

With a furor to reverse
The back of time, begins to manifest

(Stranger yet, it honeycombs their hill)
Ephesians tucked by friend or family in.

Seven troughs of stone. So the dead were baked –
El pueblo unido – soon to scowl or grin,

Being vaguely seen, wind-wrinkled shoals.
Quicker spirits hear their call drift up

Whenever those who sing along awake
Drink liquid amber or Saint Paul's bliss.

Far western winds, get this, you cornucopias
Of shooting iron, atom bomb, and Indian bone:

Violent blue above them still balloons
With small mercies, welcome, or a ship.

Then why erase these rough hewn records:
Hope sounds in a voice but not for ever.

Night Wedding in Anamur

Cézanne made men to play bézique
    You look at heavy backs
A hatted peasant head
    Perhaps a pipe gone out
Bonehard still though fathoms deep
    The wily roosters winged by hazard
Shine in the cottage empire of paint

All that was a scene will change
    The table on a shore collects
A foreign gaze a touch far out
    A table clothed in Turkish white
Seven people sitting at it
    Finger rings and tulip heads
Formal around the bowl of salt

Now let the scene unfold their flesh
    Night opens wide its cobalt mouth
Smoke and smells are tucked away
    So black the ovals cane sombreros blow
Across the sand they taste of olive

A fresher wind can levitate them now
    It has them float
The fish mothering sea that never wastes
    A breath when day dawns or doomed
Civilizations cut their bonds to fall apart
    That selfsame sea poises on its crests

Musicians busy thoughtful witnesses
    A heartbeat above
The old as usual unrolling ocean scrolls
    Now mold the air with such sweet force
Again the table lifts and dancers
    Leaping coupled skim the water

Bathed in her moon the bride
   Heavenly arms outspread
Dances to the upbeat
   And she so startled looking like a corpse
Strung with fairylights and coppery balloons
   Still quickening Attis torn and underground

Her table is upheld
   Ghosts around it eating fast
(Softly out of her silken box she rose)
   With lamb and water melon
Froth of beer still ticking in the glasses
   Each a singular shadow out

Circle

They all run around the doorstep
They point at the sky
And for sure the stars are falling
So many it's like the tassles
Of an oldtime dancing dress

But why look
When lost in thought
Inside

Why, if someone you are thinking about
Once in a house long gone without a trace
Might be recalling now
The way rain would start to patter
Across the timbered roof

And in the palm of her hand
How the dog's muzzle felt
The wet nose clean
The tongue warm

Ballad of Charlotte

Before she bought the knife to kill Marat,
Charlotte Corday had bought a fancy hat.

The five-inch knife she bought at a hardware store;
The hat was black with ribbons green galore.

At a hardware store she bought the five-inch knife,
Resolved to take the gutter tyrant's life.

She bought the hat to do the thing in style,
With a sort of Norman Mona Lisa smile.

Consider, when you visualize the scene –
Over his lukewarm bath she had to lean:

What if across her eyes the hat had slipped,
Unsighting her the moment when she gripped

Violently the knife, to push it in?
Or if the hat had fallen past her chin

And plopped, before she pushed, into the water…
Marat and Charlotte both dissolved in laughter.

Due to her sense of style it was not so;
She does for history what she had to do.

Out of her dress she takes the knife – one thrust,
Her blade has pierced his body, as it must.

Later the questions. Charlotte acted 'alone'.
Was 'firm' and 'feminine'. Conspirators? None.

Her motive? Folks, I struck the monster dead
To frighten other monsters off, she said.

Marat, mean-spirited, vindictive, shrill
Poseurs like you defraud the hungry still.

Ranting fanatics cast you as a martyr.
If only Charlotte's hat had hit the water.

Charlotte instead is later to be seen
Riding a cart on the way to the guillotine.

Behind the cart, voices sang a song,
Tiny voices heard, but not for long.

The scarlet robe she wore, without her hat,
Showed all her body's curves. Now why was that?

Pelting rain had soaked her to the skin,
No doubt to purify her of her sin.

Whose were the voices? Little girls, they say,
Held hands and sang and danced for that Charlotte Corday.

A Farewell in Old Mexico

Perhaps her husband was the engineer.
Palm up, timing perfect,
She waves to him a hazel wave.
Here is the hand she cups, at the limit

Of an arm's curve, to catch his sooty kiss.
Animal black complex of intestines
Afloat on a thunderhead of steam, to the clank
Of twenty open trucks, you expelled

A hiss. Soon the sunflower field of faces
Lifts as one to swallow cool sierra air.
Wind sang star patterns into the grit.
On the boardwalk begonias inhabit tin cans;

Liquid, they are mirrored, even redder
In the sweat beading her top lip. The caboose
A dot, now she waves, with her comical
Sense of order, to it, not him.

The Balcony Tree

New neighbour say: hope it won't interrupt you
When I walk by your open door?
O no, I say: I'm really not a rat,
At least not so you'd notice. Spring and Fall
Open is the way I like to leave it.

Hung, too, from the balcony tree a bird feeder.
New neighbour say she like it, kinda neat.
Little tree in leaf now. We
Hope this alley cat won't find
Ways to catch a finch, or me, the rat.

We say: before we open doors, we'll watch
For finch or sparrow. If they be there,
We won't step out to do the things we do.
Won't switch on our sensitive ignitions.
Try not to scare the creatures from the tree...

Must say, though, I miss
The earlier neighbour, long before
I chained the feeder to a branch.
Miss her mad look, her finger tapping window,
Clothes gone, I miss the skin, the Latin

Nipples in the candlelight,
Miss the swoop and sweat of her sassy back,
Her talk, till she took off, still going on.
Did she find work, make a buck
Where she went, with her perfumes, to look for it?

Or is she fat in San Antonio and fed up?
Who else betrayed her, made her?
Under the tree, with a low hopeless laugh
She coiled her hair up once like a Tarahumara.
Not so my new neighbour:

She tells me there's a gap. Events
To be explained. Touches of understanding
Shunned in fright. Her smile, like a fan
She tries to open but can't find the catch.
What can I tell her?

Jump the gap? Snail has a place to go,
Horse, quick, rumbas over copperhead?
But whole creeds have collapsed into the banks
We borrow lifetimes from, to eat
Frenzy, evacuate abstraction –

New neighbour know it all. So I say:
You made it home, and here is being –
No reverend killers ring this balcony tree,
My door, no bullet whanged it yet, I close
Only when I sleep or hear them march by.

Walking the Puppy

The poet of the abyss
Takes to walking the puppy
While scrolled waves gather shape
To pound the shore
He sees a flowing violet web whisked from the abyss
Furrow the hump of a sea shell

Gentle frenzy puppy digs
Through the salt and oil
She hopes for a smell at least of something
Her quick young claws how like the waves
How like her pelt the shooshoo of the foam

They frolic away to a dry dune
Where gulls glide on down to meet their shadows
Wind lets fly its foibles round the clock
Cooling the backs of nondescript objects

A bottle top, an inch of ocean macaroni
Yield a howling O
Yield an M for the Mothers
How can a puppy interpret such a text
Will she be able to scratch from it a whiff of the real

Soon the night, night will drift over it all
A violet web of swoops and ribbons
And giving tongue to other stars
Breath by breath Delta will begin to expand
Still with beaks to pierce the wind gulls are marking time
Others trot on twilit stilts looking pretty stupid

Even the puppy waits for the poet to catch up
Patting her head he forgets what it means to breathe
He strokes her small throat
In love with every shining grain of sand
He is hungry for her small head and kisses it

She runs in the shining, golden dog, mad with delight
Though at a distance, nervous of course
One small hand brushing the hot heavenly blood away
The other cupping her loneliness
Aphrodite walks from the waves again

The First Move

Looking through window glass at early light
Hearing the moon descend over the temple that was
Combing space I feel a surge of hot day to come
A Mustang glides to the curb and stops
The driver rolls his window down
And in my window's angle a shape so vague
Somehow it might have borrowed an absent limb
Is a man whose bent and only body spills a shadow

His tiny dog a solid sniffling at a bug I think
Still the Mustang driver through his other window
Parting foliage has to see the brick tower beyond

Has the clockwork stopped
Have they stopped their arguments and screams
Now what will the boiling corporals do
And the children too hungry to cry out

Flit of sparrow
Descending on seeds in the feeder east of me
Hand reaching out through the open Mustang window
A whole arm snaking out
The hand has touched the hot or cool car roof
The shadow on tarmac sharp as the dog's *Geruch*
Immobile as this bergamot in a smoky taste of tea
Me immobile feeling through window glass
How absently till now I have clawed at life

Unchanged the light identical the suspense
Whoever moves first will make the first move

Vietnamese Harp

Before first light awake
  At a touch on a button
One taut steel string plucked I heard
  And another, another

Penetrating the dark a music
  Of spine and thighbone
Clear as the contour of a waterlily
  Ghostly as the snow it cups

Floated from its peak
  To ground, a shimmering pagoda
Spreads and folds its wings
  Stands where I lay

Amazingly nowhere, almost
  Too much trance for a body
So soon in the day, cut loose
  From the singing zigzags

I walked outside, by the open window
  Taking the same sounds in
But curious who in spirit
  Now might weep to be listening

Saloon with Birds

If someone barefoot stood in a saloon,
His dromedary might be chomping, outside,
That majestic meal. High olive notes
Plucked from a mandolin. Fumes. Leafgreen.

A dark descends. There, with banana palm,
Consorts forbidden music. Ugly. Ocean.
Delay it. First a clatter, from the birds.
They wax decrepit. Vocal signatures:

Who could ever have so illuminated them
That the letters, cut from stark air,
Assume no solitary monumental pose,
But wavily ache with the boat hulls?

Certain or not, an urgent finger prodded
Epsilons and wagtailed gammas free
From habit, a peculiar glue. No help. No
Waste. In the saloon each dust spake.

In the saloon the spokes of another
Sunlight, still this ocular companion though,
Rolled afternoons around, like meatballs,
Bubbles of corn sizzling in a crystal pan.

Throaty owls also, they could entertain
Quick, tensile teeth. A joy. Pelican moonlit.
Look at a pine nut. It exists, you know.
Little furred insects inhabit vast smells.

For this the saloon is open. A waft.
A waft is all it takes. A venetian blind
Has wrinkled the wash basin. A cool expounds
Blood orange, air in China, appalling beliefs.

Air wraps the mast. Air singing. Air,
The solo invader who timed anew
Our free objects. The saloon twangs,
Dust swims, a gong letting its hum fly.

Closing never. Least of all on syllables.
A split lemon has released from evil
Any soul what's willing. Get that. Now
Never you move like you were shrunk to be.

Or else forgo the little sorrow. Treasure
The big one. Tell, in the saloon,
Nothing of it. Look up. Long enough
The ocean has delayed. You can breathe again.

Roma 1985

Deep underground the sewers must be breathing,
Even abominable temples not yet dug up –

There you might find on stone a wicked scribble,
Or a phrase chiselled from a cantata by Catullus.

Deep down below, the poor and foreigners believe,
A clink of gold coins in a pot can be heard.

All around our hollow now and here, dust thickens;
Pricks harden to the crack of killing gas.

So we stop indoors and eat leaves of artichoke:
Ancient nerves of the city spread such a calm in us.

Or we take short breaths and trot across a street
Winged by grappa, ballasted by chocolate ice cream.

No use. No use at all. Reverse formations dilate
The negative; stress-fed cancers nibble bone and lung.

Yet high on moneyed roofs refreshing trees grow tall,
Hyacinths commit natural acts of resistance.

Earth has to grow one more new skin, people think
Like Rumi: We are alive today with another life.

Another Almost

Almost it might be better
to forget the past than build
ruins out of ruins

Perhaps the ruins are forms
of a response too blocked or timid.
Who can figure a whole house?

Think of the first scavenging Turks,
incurious, they patched their huts
with odds and ends of temples

No, I mean it is tough going
always to remember
so little or too much

Then have it all, or some,
spring unbidden back into place.
The bundle of woe is heavy

Wave to me as I go,
inhabitants of memory,
from your ruins, houses, forests

Continue the story that broke,
somehow, in the middle.
Let me see, let me smell you

Intact to my hearing
perhaps you will open
zones of being I never knew

Mysterious flesh
might blossom, lost hills
tipped with frail churches

Mansions complete
with moats of liquid silver,
misty kitchens, whence

Incredible pastries issue, baked
in ovens I never saw,
wines I never drank

Might redden tables of real oak
in twilight courtyards –
all ordinary as now. So I bend

With an ache for you, child,
and one for you, my only love,
and another for Doyle, Irish pilot

Blown to bits on a rocket range.
More lovely or horrible
things I know

Happen to others,
I write this only to shorten
the time of a music

Which, unless I forget,
will mass ruin on ruin.
The watermill we slept in,

My other love, the rushing
water beneath us,
you had clipped my fingernails

So I forget it, forget, child,
the midnight we were frightened of.
I hoist on my back again

The bundle of woe, but first
I open it, a crack,
to see the bloody rags

And worn-out toothbrushes,
the splinters of bone
and a silver ring from Afghanistan

Which slid into a river;
I sniff the hair beside me,
I touch excited midnight skin

The time of a music
almost now I hear the spell of it
playing backwards

Lampoon

1

The man across the street I thought was mad
Is playing catch this evening with a lad.

I hear the ball he flings plop into the glove
Worn by the lad, who's husky. Is it love?

Can love have cured him for a time? Or God?
The man has dialectically changed. How odd.

2

Push it aside, the surface image. Shove
The husky lad away, the baseball glove –

Recall another scene: J. Edgar Hoover
Drooled over snapshots of his husky lover

Curled up in shorts beside a swimming pool:
O toad-cold passion of 'The Heat' – how cool!

3

My madman, in the winter, scarlet cap
Pulled down around his eyes, I saw him tap-

Dance in the street and scatter in the snow
His brownbag lunch along the wall below

For hungry birds. Once he told me, too,
He used to live right here, where I now do.

4

Then off he crawled. The scarlet cap has gone,
Now shirt tail flaps, his left foot settles on

The broken ground, he lets the baseball fly,
Slow, to be sure, but straight enough. While I

Have scandalous doubts – the lad, is he his son?
Kinsman, or neighbour? Is he his illusion? –

The fact remains that in the USA
It's hard to know, harder still to say.

5
My madman plays the heretic, for once,
If blind Greed is the God of North Americans.

The corpse of instinct spits, when pressed by sport,
A lethal wad into the face of thought:

Yet, healed by sport, not love, that heretic
Can't quench the appetites that make him sick –

Captive of the Social Lie, him too. Down goes
His foot and up the dubious ball he throws.

6
So civilization plays to thwart all dreams:
The depth of life won't surface here, it seems.

He's mad as Hoover still, huffpuffing a sane
Picture of himself, while, yet again

The ball or switch is flicked, the rockets go:
There'll be no scandal. Not a soul will know.

Empty Fifth

Des Lebens Überfluß, das Unendliche,
Das um ihn   und dämmert, er faßt es nie.
Hölderlin, 'Rousseau'

That was in music
    This is not
The empty fifth
    A few folks thought

When flesh was colour
    Poxes death
Soldiers soldiered
    Taxes rose

And queens might rip
    In fat châteaux
Being bored to tears
    Their robes for a song

To be a presence
    Tongue can touch
Or keep from trickling
    Through to nought

Is not your own
    Near-empty fifth
A bottle of Scotch
    In a foul motel

Not medieval
    Sad to say
No meaning wink
    To flash at God

But back it brings
    A mason's pick
Plenitude of stone
    An oak floorboard

Or else in a daze
    Of infant bliss
A fishing pond
    Delays for a bit

By noon becalmed
    The nose of a stag
A vagabond girl
    Who cools her quim

Strategic towns
    Roll off the map
If anything stops
    Remember time

So portals open
    Pilgrims can yawn
Tulips to the wind
    Toss their pollen

And leather smells
    In a barn of stars
To split all reason
    Spin the glass

With one last swig
    Suppress a groan
The best revolution
    Skin and bone

Cool Places

The scene may be water.
Still on some branches,
Radiant with impulse,
An avalanche of almond
Settles in mid-air.

Or smoke may be the scene.
Tugged sideways by wind,
Blue masks, half history for ever,
Spiral off the sensitive
Backbones of horses.

A little love goes far,
Fine words nowhere.
Something unbroken in people –
Spirits murmur round it.
Suddenly ancient an embrace

Speeds intelligence. I broke
Pattern, breathe to attract you:
Speak, if well-being was
Ever by any speech-act
Driven into the script we are.

Or be done with it. See the zebra
Stand its ground, cascades
Happily freshen high beliefs.
Old men want more
Than rumours of women.

Cool places, good cool places
Exist, not far, where
For wasting your life
You are forgiven. What horrors next?
What presences wither in the air?

All It Was

It might be good
To think it did not matter much.
All the way we'd come;
Where had we got to now?

The brisk blue shadows
Nestling in the sheet,
The birthmark on your spine
A forked cloud from a squid,

Still they pointed a way
On and on to an elsewhere
Breath alone, breathing alone
Perhaps could reach.

But into you I leaned
And felt a trembling go
From all my body out
Into your sudden sleep.

Then it was my hand
Moved from your shoulderblade
Up to rest a while
Where your front meets your back

On a ridge where
Like thunder your black
Curls hang and flash –
Not that it matters much.

Next your fingers came;
Proceeding out of your sleep,
They took my hand and held
All of us, warm, in the light.

Tristia ex Provincia

Twenty times in the night a horse ran past
My hidden house. When I looked
I saw a head and back and hoofs;
All the articulations in between
Were solid flesh, the heartbeat of a horse.

It ran between the olive and the broom,
While in Berlin people took to the streets,
Shouted their disbelief at the police
And brought a dismal system crashing down.
Between the olive and the broom it ran

Doing what comes freely to a horse:
Blubbering out through lips an oaty breath,
Or stationary, tossing a mane at the moon.
Whenever I got up I shook with fright,
I pinched myself when I lay down again.

What had called to the horse, what did it want?
Not to be not contained or simply dead;
Thigh to ear the long thrust of a backbone,
And in pitch dark the scent of hay, on hard
Beaten earth, on rock, the ring of hoofs.

A rush of shadow, beat of wings, me shaking still
With fright whenever I got up to see,
All night the horse was drumming back and forth.
It ran between the olive and the broom,
No rush of air, no beat of wings, still shaking me.

The Headland

Beyond the shacks where food is sold
Beyond the booths haunted by carpet men
Beyond the goats and stone lidded broken tombs
Look the headland

How many times have you seen it there
Not knowing if it had a place in time
Thinking you had seen it only in a dream

Beyond any imaginable midpoint of the world
Memory brimmed unbidden with whole colours
Only to end in a choking dust of names

But answering your body which stores light as it can
Answering rhythms that curl but cling to nothing at all
Rhythms given flesh for a measure to feel with

The track goes on up the shoulder of the headland
Saffron earth anchored by rock
Storm torn rock walls to clamber over at the top

How many times did you see from there
Sheltered in a bay the next village
Fishermen stooping at the prow to pull the anchor up
It would have taken a lifetime to get there
How many lifetimes to the city of emerald and snow

How many times hearing a mast creak
Hum of rope drawn taut and dripping
Did you look back to see the headland disappear

Shoe soles worn thin by long walks
Pierced by the long thorns
Then barefoot and kneedeep in the sea
Hardly ever any deeper
In your dented helmet or coonskin cap
There today again and glad but not to be alone
Shading your eyes you will have seen the headland

Stele in Istanbul

The dead man beckons to a water melon
Out of the water melon a big slice was bitten
A cup of clay in his hand he beckons in fact
To the naked wine boy not the water melon
To the naked wine boy he beckons
And wags his beard for he means to speak

However the cup is made of stone
Stone the melon the dead man looks at
Easily it could be the moon at third quarter
A moon to tell what time of night or day
What corner of a lifetime the man died at

Not a corner nor a wrinkle on him the wine boy
Still to make you shiver touches polished his limbs
Any moment now he will dip his jar
Into the big stone wine pot

And erect in her palm a woman holds a corn cob
Back of the man who beckons to the stone water melon moon
Her right hand appeases the stone air above the corn cob
Gently she wishes to protect the thing
Or else the stone caught her in the act of spinning
So the corn cob never was a corn cob but a spool

While blue fish still flourish in this Golden Horn
A greyhound whirls his behind under the dead man's bed
That was how he'd welcome the dead man home
The shades are biting now suppose the man said
But part of me hangs on though the spool stops
Only the dog saw how spent he was from not willing
The known stone thing and the water melon moon

Titian's *Venere Giacente*

Not a moment too soon: quit of her gowns the lady
Positions herself on the chaise longue
And has crossed her shins; her left hand,
The little finger ringed, cups her sex.
Behind the flower pot with a shrub in it
A curtain of blue is coming down from heaven;
The tree and the glowing Corinthian column
Break a gold horizon. It is nine:
Time for something to happen.

Not a moment too soon the spaniel hopped up
And curled on the crumpled
Yellow sheet that covers the chaise longue.
He is already pretending to sleep and the little girl
Pretends to be praying at the window seat;
Her nurse, rolling a sleeve up, pretends
To be saying 'Honey, come, it's time for your bath,
And what are you doing, pray as you must,
Growing that fine young bottom in your snowy dress?'

Next, as above, not a moment too soon
The smile stole as prescribed
To the lady's lips and turned their corners up.
She is looking at you, in wonder.
Because she is looking at you, lightly her right hand
Toys with a formal bouquet somebody else left;
Hair loose on her well developed shoulder
Falling to cover the armpit somebody else
Knew was unbelievably tender,
Must be soft, cool to the touch; the sun has spread
First light in it for a fawn to step,
Scenting berries, into its coppery glade.

Now she arranges her whole look.
The head tilts, the virginal face finds an angle
To size you up and bring you on
Like a dish so foreign she's hardly curious,
Yet now, not a moment too soon,
At last she is tasting it, then devours it,
Faster and faster, more and more.

                    What is the snag?
Why hesitate? The black screen blotting out
All but these three quarters of the picture
Is only there to sharpen the lady's outline.
You are only invited to admire,
Surging out of the dark, or actually not so,
Yet it resists the dark, a wave continuous
From shoulder to hip, and a forearm, limp,
There, rested on the hip bone:
A rosy organ, fingered, freed from the very dark,
Which, by the way, also confirms the upturn
Of one breast.
                    Did you expect the screen not to cut
The window in half, not to segregate
Light the window admits like a last whisper,
From the candle blaze that has mysteriously
Clarified the lady's abandon in her undreamed flesh?

Or were you of a mind there should be
A picture in it,
Not this nothing at all that is not even a prop,
A picture of a mirror reflecting a lady
In a mirror reflecting a picture of now you know what?

Go in there. Make friends. She will know when
To shuffle off the dog and pull the black screen
All the way across.

The Clothes Moth

Little as the fingernail of a ten-year-old,
You have the shortest whiskers of a cat.

Up close, easily seen in the slant light,
Two profiles merge, like rivers, across your wings;

And the face of a Chinese emperor is disclosed,
Smiling, moth, on your Mesopotamian back.

Outlined against the pinewood table top
Your shape is less fan, less tulip

Than the Egyptian lotus with tornado lips
They hammered into drachmas on Cyprus once.

So much abstruse cutting of throats then,
Now the history scatters in a golden dust

I catch my breath at, when your whiskers twitch.
A breath lofted you, now gone you are,

Yet I think you might have been there always,
There no less than fingers I will fork to grip

The cigarette, than wine still black in a bottle.
What if now I saw the design on my own back?

What rivers, what profiles, what bloodshed
Might melt into a design to be misread,

As if through valley mist, by a yokel pretending
To an imperfect, imaginary intelligence?

Cloaked in provocative scrawls the globe
Throws to the winds the grids we put around it.

So, in the moment of this furor, you took off:
You wisely muscled in to my thin stock of wool;

Now I hear your soft jaws munch my blanket.
So I became your fleece and you my Argonaut.

2

Note. Huapango – a Mexican dance-song of Caribbean origin, in which the dance steps of a couple alternate between trampling on one spot and hopping in a low arc to trample on another spot. Junius Avitus – died young, soon after becoming a senator, a protégé of Pliny the Younger, who loved him for his promise, his meticulous hard work, his willingness to learn (*Letters*, VIII, 23).

A Huapango for Junius Avitus

*Accedit lacrimis meis quod absens et
impedentis mali nescius, pariter aegrum
pariter decessise cognovi, ne gravissimo
dolori timore consuescerem.*

Pliny the Younger

1

Stepping out from the new Bangkok Café
Digesting the whitest
Meat of spicy chicken

Night hawk heard aloft
Orbiting the ventilators
Of Congress Avenue, this hot hot gulch

His high, strangled cry
A soprano raspberry
Reminding me of Rossini

Whom ice cream polished off
Boom – how come I slow down slightly
Firefly from split concrete winking

Cooks, octets and chickens
How come I slow down at all
All too soon will have had their fill of me

Boomboom boom – unwinding silver ladder
None too soon
Mysterious dame thou penetratest me.

2

Staring at the moon a cat thinks
It is a dish of milk

The cat staring at the moon
Wants to include it somehow

It might be cheese with a mouse
Tremendously creeping up on it

I'll wait and see, the cat declares
The same as I say this about the cat

The urge is there: live without knowing how
Idea is there: for building shrouded systems

Tear off the sheet: what's there is featured
Stone or a royal sport of the unconscious

A point in time – rounded arms reaching out
With heat but no direction, say Come over here

Your aftershave is nice, I'll risk the consequences
Vague, outside, still the traffic roars

At leisure sea shells unwind their echoing forms
Silver in the moonlight fox fur crackles

And crystal fleets whizz oblivious across the bridge
Their juggler, hands behind his back, distracted

A point in time split into infinitely small
Sensitive fibres could tomorrow resume

Existence as a hero, scribbled fish: I exist
Like everybody, waiting for a rhyme or crash

To work the change, a crisis freshening the sun
Yet suppose the sea shell, suppose the idea

Unqualified create only to disregard
Those singular fables which invent the cat

Uncontainable web, trembling with just what?
Whatever frenzy knits bones, whatever tenderness

Desires you to speak, on me your lingo's lost
You might pronounce wrath, or mercy, or both

You might shield me with ignorance
Rage at me for love I want to shake you with –

And how apt, settling under the baobab, the leopard
A dervish hat completes the cook who plays the spoons

3
You turn right
    at the second sign, soon, at the crossways
        of a bridge and a sea shell
            continue left to the cook
and straight ahead to the rhomboid of distraction

You will find a wing there
    and a corkscrew ascent
        to a second bridge. Do not miss the egg,
            clearly marked, you have been there before
and the lights give out, see, just before the dip

There is a field of cows,
    you pass it on the left. Observe
        the pylon, like a picked
            albacore backbone; if you stop
you'll hear the wind bellow in it, likely as not

Later, left at the fork
    and follow the loop. You smell woodsmoke
        if you're on track. Slow down
            at Silken Ladder, circle
Cat Lagoon, then back off and sleep some

There's a tidy walk ahead;
    the path is one you won't miss.
        Cobwebs will catch your shoes and face,
            the first aren't poison, but watch
for the purple ones, the stickiest, they mean forget

The Greater Evil.
   Now all the sounds will keep you
      wide awake: the nosing, quibblous, of the fong,
         click of bullwits, the oom's horn.
You'll soon tune in. Forward to the fork, here,

Or there, for the nth time,
   you have to decide –
      stop till sunup, or fail –
         plod on, dance with your telescope, tongs,
your feathering tool, your grip of loose leaves –

Plod on, soon you'll see the
   gap in the boob trees.
      Then (inaudible words)
         (more inaudible words)
Brisk wind foretold it, boom, the unshrouded sea

Here all things turn
   their backs on you. Nothing
      watches you. Now it is too late
         to save your precious skin, it's
listening the other way, as if to another voice

The load of *la matière*
   and feelings that attach to it,
      the great dusts, groans, the golightly trees
         turn inside out, reform into a hole
and in the hole (involved, turning its back on you –

Or can it be Death Mountain?) moment dwells.
   Let everything go, gaze at it,
      as long as it is there, the moment hole.
         Never think all time is abuzz in it.
Never put your eye so close you could be blown away

By the grace it is giving out, pulse
   never spent, of carnal
      starlight a fountain, supposing earth
         and you, if ever again, eye to eye with a beak-
to-flower hummingbird, can figure time like that

4

Soon is a kind of never in reverse
Save when a phrase's gist is negative
Soon you'll die just when you want to live
A cry from Never posits to disperse

Spun like a top in umpteen kinds of time
Configured as in music or more flat
As lurching on from this dull urge to that
Ugly history leaves a trail of slime

A soon that could be now the future past
Emergent time tormenting in the rose
Skipping an aeon if the ground's too hot

Ah incandescent now again outlast
Soons that never sang a note but froze
To dwindle on the tips of tongues forgot

5

My heron has flown into the blue night wood
My sparrow into the perpendicular dust
My falcon, better than my wrist, loves the sky

What shall I do, mysterious dame, with this thought
It has angles and nodes I know nothing of
I am not very well acquainted yet with the dark

I am not afraid of the night wood, nor of dust
And I love the sky no less than my falcon does
With a pinch of salt I eat food as I need it

Also I hear in corners floorboards creak
As if somebody trod behind the shadows there
But I do not collect my times into a pattern

I do not work things out or drink white milk
Because white things are impersonating me
A white horn in a corner blows for a minute

A white horn in a corner when the creaking stops
Spreads a vista of stone gates and streaming hair
In an ancient city where I met you sometime

And the city to come is a far cry from my thought
The generation of thought a far cry from reason
When I see my falcon's face I am not in doubt

There are skies
There are dusts
There are losses we bear as best we can

There is an old book on the demons I might read
There is a new face to love, which I do not choose
There is a distraction from things and anxieties

It is for instance distracting to know this or that
And how not knowledge hurts but experience
And how you live, mysterious dame, in death

It is distracting never to be disenchanted
To have the spring of joy always bubbling up
To be sad without any thought of sadness

Distracting to be told your sadness was intended
Sadness the snout of a weapon pointed at life
Heron, sparrow, falcon falling from the sky

The tone, of an unfingered string
The fluidity, now, of the flight
The going on of everything at your ancient behest

Come to me again with understanding some other time

3

The Matter of History

Somewhere I have lost a description. It was an eyewitness description of an incident during the three-way battles between Poles, White and Red Russians which laid Galicia waste during the summer and autumn of 1920. If I could characterize the moments at which my thoughts return to the description, I might be able to tell what is at the back of this loss. The texture of such moments, if I could at least recall them, might be so repaired as to unfold before me again the entire description, lacking not a word. As it is, when versions of the scene itself occur to me, without any trace of the original text, I cannot capture even the qualities of those moments.

In one version of the scene, while everywhere bullets are flying and across the alleys, up and down muddy streets in a small Galician town haggard Hasids in caftans and frightened capless children are scampering, while women scream and slam doors behind them, artillery shells sporadically crash into already quaking façades, through smoking roofbeams, a clown is being treated to a funeral. All the horses have been commandeered, so the funeral cart is dragged by two burly men: their fists gripping the shafts glisten with rain. The open coffin bounces in the cart and in the coffin is the dead clown, white-faced and shock-headed, his red bubble nose and arched black eyebrows apparently sheltered by death, for not one bullet even grazes the cart. You can just see the red nose bobbing up and down at eye-level as the cart squishes through the mud and jolts over the cobblestones.

There is one moment, now I come to think of it, at which this version is changed again, reconfigured in memory, and that is the moment in which I remember another funeral, a second one. In 1577 two mischievous boys thrust a lighted taper through a peep hole in the rear wall of the great sarcophagus in Ravenna, where, in full regalia, the very sporting Roman Empress Galla Placidia had sat enthroned, dominating her basilica, for a thousand years, and blew her up – every shred of mould, bone and brocade, every cobweb, every mouse's toothmark, consumed in a sheet of flame.

These two scenes disperse all awareness of the actual circumstances in which they return to me, unconjured, unbidden. If I could restore the circumstances, then the qualities of the moments in which the scenes return might flood my memory afresh; I would be content with no more than a trickle. As it is, the circumstances and the qualities of the moments remain buried, buried in me like Attila in the Danube, encased in a triple coffin: Attila in a gold one, the gold one in a silver one, the silver one in an iron one. For a story goes that his Huns, having contrived to build a dam, dug a channel and diverted a stretch of the Danube for just as much time as it took to sink the coffins into the bed of the Danube.

It is difficult not to believe that, if it is possible to speak of history on the whole, the whole of history, hostile as it is to any single or social body that constitutes it, is deviation, and that whatever borders we may gropingly prescribe for it, in our craving for descriptions, lost or found, old or new, the most the least deluded do is knit together rafts and float them out, like texts on paper, in a willing disbelief that they will not founder on currents of time which respond, below devouring drifts, to a continuum so secret that every surge in it, vast or private, every climax even, must increase the degree of deviation and propel its curve just long and far enough for it to be perceived afresh the instant it transforms itself into the finite enveloping contour of a foetus, a foetus not yet ready to answer (still crossing the starlit spaces interior to its own mass) the call to be born.

Muzaffar and Mutadid

The story goes that in Andalusia around the middle of the eleventh century, after the disappearance of the great Omayyad khalifs, after the aborted people's revolution in Cordova, after the gardens and palaces of Abd-er-Rahman III and Ibn Khattab el-Almanzor had been destroyed and the fabulous library of Hakam II torched and dispersed, two tyrants found themselves fighting tooth and nail. First there were many skirmishes, warnings, defeats and victories, burnings of crops, bodies mutilated, mothers and spike-tongued horses screaming. Then to Muzaffar of Badajoz came the news that the allegedly vast army of Mutadid of Seville had massacred his Berber allies and that the severed head of their commander, the young prince of Cramona, had been presented to Mutadid. A notable collector of heads, Mutadid had laid the prince commander's in a coffer beside that of the prince's grandfather.

Yet Muzaffar feigned indifference. Anon he sent to Cordova for some singing girls. Only two could be found, and those quite mediocre, yet he bought them. This whim of his caused some surprise, for the King of Badajoz was reputed to be a serious and even studious man. The surprise ceased when his motive was found out. At the estate sale of a deceased Cordovan vizier, Mutadid had bought one renowned songstress. As if to show how detached he could be, Muzaffar acquired at another sale not one singing girl but two. They might not be renowned, but might they not exceed the distinction of merely one by combining their degrees of mediocrity? Would not Muzaffar acquire thereby a reputation for detachment equal at least to that of bull-headed Mutadid?

Then the real question arose. The continuous noise, heat, and dust of battle – behind it many decades of carnage, lethal treachery, rape, crucifixions, border disputes and economic changes – had made anyone's chance of survival so tenuous, life so rare, grief so futile, that those kings, who were supposed to be enormous barns of life, towering silos of inexhaustible energy that could duly trickle down to the weavers and potters, scriveners and scribes, even down to the hairy little men with hoes in orchards, had to show that they were still intact. What clearer proof could they offer than a willingness to listen, come dusk or dawn, to the voices of singing girls?

So Muzaffar had tried to go one better than Mutadid. Mutadid may have shown superior vitality by vanquishing Muzaffar in battle and by gazing, rapt, into the vacant eyeballs of the prince of Cramona, but Muzaffar bought two, not one but two singing girls, to whose voices, not renowned but mediocre, he might henceforth listen, as long as he was not dead, with detachment. I'll get him yet, that bull-head, he must have muttered to himself, I don't think they're mediocre at all, in fact I never did hear nary a one of them miss a note or skip a word. Let others carp and say they got real squeaky voices, or flabby ones, and that I got me a raw deal, I don't think so, and after another cup or two of this wine, over-oaky as it is, and sour as a mule's ass, they'll sing all the sweeter.

Mutadid meanwhile, back in Seville, knew he had Muzaffar over a barrel now. The mediocrities in Badajoz were his signal to proceed with negotiations: Muzaffar was evidently capable of compromise. With those negotiations out of the way, he scowled at his renowned songstress, I can do what they'll say I did – turn my spears against Ibn Yahyâ of Niebla and that affluent little islander 'Abd al-'Aziz the Bakrite.

August 1939

The cool of sea water circles arched bare feet exploring jagged rock pool floors and invades the fingerbones of one hand spread to collect, before it rolls away, shifted by water gushing through a cleft in the rock, or by the slipstream of the hand descending, a small cowrie shell.

The shell is grooved and ridged. Like mercator latitudes across a globe shrunk to the mass of a child's knuckle, grooves and ridges run over its hump and stop at a sort of lip. Here's the slit, on the shell's underside. You peer into it. The cavity inside, imaginably lived in, scented with salt, lit by a far darker sun, whichever way you tilt it, calls to you from beyond any angle of vision, any pressure of a fingertip.

Across sand, all of it pulverized rock and shell, they said, barefoot to the path. Along the path, smell of bracken bitter green, and to the footsoles marked by smudges of tar, imprints of grass, usually patches of wet sand stuck for a while. Now step across the stream, on flat stones.

Small shade trees slant across the stones. Sunlight outlines frail liquid wings that lift to propel the stream past the bluish lower contours of its stones. Honestly no way goes through the surfaces, no way around them. Hardest, sanely to absorb the shock of meeting, head-on, breathless, having caught up with them, things that can't stop.

Something enormous, nameless, gradual, time and again it collects like fingers into a fist, loosening a storm you run to shelter from. It throbs and grips in the cold that makes hands hurt and blue. It coils in driftwood, tideline, oily corpse of a cormorant; air booming in your ears when you shoot, with a splutter, through a wave, what force expands the wave – could you walk into it, float with it, wash in it? Why do they forget it, pretend it isn't there?

A bell tent breathes in and out, a gust of wind from the sea, an open flap, a loose cord whacks the canvas just once. A table and two camp beds model the space inside, where a paraffin lamp has not yet been lit. The twilight contained in the tent has a glow of its own. Mackerel are frying in oil. Supper first and then, father puffing his summer pipe, cocoa and a game of cards.

Not far, the gasps of the sea. On another fringe of thought another neighbourhood, other people. Their tents dot the valley. Secluded in one of them, a tall hawk-faced man is taking notes for the tenth chapter of his reasonably natural treatise on the eye-teeth sentry, they said. In our mackerel tent it's Cheyney we read, rummy we play. Somebody says 'Poland' and always smells of the same soft banana.

Floating back across the stream in the onset of dark a boy's features leaf through smells and temperatures, night's Indian adventure, there's a hollow in the chest, in every tendon an urge, vague, to explode, but his nose is sunburned, his eyes Chinese. With a florin in his pocket, he craves to become something, something between, between a detective and a fisherman. Possibly his owl is getting ready to hoot now; its eyes open wide with a click. Rubbed between his palms a stalk of green bracken creaks, then splits, filling with a glint of puppy yelps, a wheeling twitter of linnets, the owl's impenetrable glass, then with a breath everything is erased. A joy. A fear.

That sinister throb, heard behind the song mother sang, old Greek words in her little girl's voice, comes from the engines of armed submarines burrowing now toward the Atlantic. There will be a war, but she said it's fine to sleep, if you must, with the sea in earshot.

Mongolian Breakfast

A case of isolated conscience, it is amusing, the feast in full cry, flight of boiled hens down the throats and tables, dim lights hung low, no, kerosene lamps with stems of brass, the conversation a tapenade of Gregorian chant and hyenas, only the pepper is quartz, the wines electric and half the music a wobble of minims driven off by the artillery barrage of cork, talk, bones cracking, truffles dislocated.

The tawny Pole, behind his lamp, scrambling up the slopes of a volcano of vodka, does not mind the hammering from carpenters, storms of newly mixed cement being spooned into bowls by a hod-carrying waiter; isolated conscience he is saying as he turns to face the camera, as if it were a disease, the conscience or the camera, each in his outlook is both.

Anomaly, he asks, but without question, an amusing anomaly. Is it one single conscience, isolated but radiant in a Mongolia of corruption, boiled hen, a clove of garlic stuck in your hollow tooth, fated as a duck, moiré as a phenomenon, or do I tax your Polish? If otherwise, then it is not isolated, could a conscience be so, without withering like a village, no, it is plain bad.

At which moment, isolated and conscient, with a flow of joints, the rag doll dances across this diningroom, a smile creasing her flat face, one eyelid flapping loose. Reassurance. So she dances, stitched at neck, knee and elbow with silk, flipflop, a songbook between her pink chipolata fingers, and laced to her back with bacon rinds a guitar carved out of horse meat, mine, yours.

When she tries to speak, all that comes from her trembling rainbow lip is a tiny gasp, end-stopped with a hiccup, which the Polish gentleman rewards, the dog, tilting his glass, with a wink.

A Moment in the Eighteenth Century

Deep down in the shadows of Joseph-Ignace Guillotin's imagination lay the negative of his positively perfect design. Man of science that he was, prone as he was to raising at the drop of a hat a theory of hats that dropped, he had always proceeded, without ever noticing the singular motion of shadows at his feet, wherever he walked or rode, with both eyes blinking at the pitfalls. His technically perfect design, later to be realized in prototype by a melancholy German piano maker, was only drawn during a fit of abstraction after he had dreamed one night. All night he had dreamed (so he thought, when he woke) and dreaming he had composed from the shadows of his imagination a comprehensive picture of pitfalls rarely glimpsed (so various they were) in a world where everything stood the wrong way up.

In his dream there had been company, but he had not known whose. A perfectly round hole, only three inches in diameter, had appeared in the parquetry floor. Or had the parquetry been grass, or a sheet of solid rock? He could not be sure. Out of curiosity he had inserted into this unbidden hole a glove, an odd glove he had found about his person. First he had ascertained that the glove was neither one of a pair, nor inside out. Together with his company he then peered into the hole and observed that the palm of the glove jackknifed, the wilted fingers fattened, rigid for an instant, then an inexplicable suction from below plucked the glove, palm, fingers, and wrist, like a malformed fruit, out of the visible world.

Sound there had been none. Nor did M. Guillotin shudder in his dream. The thought came to him that, just as this hole had opened in the parquetry (grass, or rock), so it might open in any place, at any time. This was the thought that crossed his mind, and then a breeze ruffled the curtains. He looked past his company and saw, outside, the sun for a moment catching the tiles on the far side of the courtyard, a black sheen flashing across the crown of the coachman's hat as a heavy coach rolled into the courtyard.

When he looked down at the hole again, it had deepened. It was a cylinder. The perfectly round cylinder was dimly illuminated; and as he gazed down into it, the light, or glow, of the cylinder was just sufficient for M. Guillotin to discern a tiny glove, visible afresh and perfectly intact, resting on the bottom. This reassured him; but now, now the bottom began to sink, opening, and the glove sank along with it, the glove, tinier still, until, not a sound to be heard, another distracting gust of air ruffled the curtains. He risked another look. The cylinder was now dizzyingly deep. There was no sign at all of the glove.

He turned to his company. He asked his company: What do you make of that? His company was quite unmoved: Of what?

Of the hole and the glove and the disappearance of the glove in the ever deepening hole that has now become a cylinder, a perfect cylinder descending through the foundations into the earth and down which (M. Guillotin added with slow emphasis) not only gloves but whole houses, horses, cities and civilizations, nay, the frozen glory of Newtonian space itself... He stopped. His company was adjusting the curtains, now they fell in straight folds from their wooden rod to the skirting board, where a pinch of fluff began to swirl.

Looking back to the hole once more, M. Guillotin saw that its diameter was increasing. With the utmost caution he extended a forefinger, at his own height, into the air, above the hole. He felt a cool draught, heard an inhalation, as of excitement, and quickly withdrew his finger. The sound, which had begun as a gasp, ended as a sigh. The expansion of the diameter, even then, was arousing his curiosity. There was not only a hole with a cylinder continuously deepening and still faintly glowing, there was now an extension of the cylinder up through the parquetry, grass, rock, pavement, with a wall that was now perfectly tubular but terraced like the interior of an antique amphitheatre. What if the activity in and of the hole might not be imitating, as on a stage, all the past and future people? What might be the intrigue, what the drift, of such a drama? In a moment he had taken a seat, and sitting there he felt perfectly comfortable. He sat and watched.

This was the point at which his company took up a position in the open window and blocked the passage of light into the room. The fluff was still swirling, the curtains falling in their straight folds, but M. Guillotin noticed that the parquetry was crowding in on him, closer and closer, while the diameter of the hole elastically expanded to accomodate the mass of his body and the cylinder performed its evidently automatic action. With some alarm he pondered what reasonable measures he might take to extricate himself and continue to observe events from his usual height in relation to the parquetry.

Easing first one buttock, then the other, upwards, heaving himself thus, or, like a frigate, rolling, he contrived to resist the seduction of the amphitheatre and, with a last nimble twist, to free his whole body. A close call, he reflected. A moment more and it might have been too late. Then came the panic.

In his panic he walked rapidly, with tiny steps, almost childlike, to the window and besought his company to notice what had been going on. Now what do you make of that? he asked, straightening his breech flap, which had been skewed by his exertions. His company leaned against the window frame, gazed out into the courtyard. A maid was crossing it, carrying a pail of milk to the kitchen annexe. She walked with a slight limp.

When M. Guillotin looked back into the room, the hole, still active, was giving out a sound like stage thunder, a rustled rattling, the shaking of a thin, shining, tin tray. Listen to that, he said. They want more, they always want more: for a second time his company had spoken. Who are they? M. Guillotin asked. Who always wants more?

He said this to himself while he was waking up. As he woke up he also remembered one more detail: the stage thunder had been accompanied by a rising, inside the cylinder and flush with its wall, of a silvery cap, a solid surface, which would soon lie flush with the parquetry too, perfectly smooth. He reflected that this smooth and silvery flush fit would be admired by all, as indeed much that is believed to be continuous is admired amid the reversals of the manifest world.

The Image

When they finally got around to where they had begun, it wasn't there any more. This was because they'd strung it out behind them. What had been a chariot of fire had become a rickety old wooden wagon. Losing its parts as it bumped along, wheels breaking, then dropping off, the rest of it a carcass of broken axles, bleached boards, rusted prongs and rotted leather cinches, it had eventually, without anyone noticing when it happened, disconnected itself, then vanished into thin air. It would have made not a scrap of difference if someone had been delegated to keep an eye on it, down the years. They never should have hitched it up, to be hauled behind them, in the first place. So now they looked around, checking the latitude. Forgetfully they wondered where it might have gone. Might they have miscalculated their position? Had they drifted or been driven off course? There had been hazards, they could have been driven off course; they could have drifted, there had been spates of negligence. But no, they had arrived at the exact same spot, this was where they'd begun. There were no signs of the four rivers, no views of the mountain. As for the temperate climate some of the old hands had spoken of, now there came over them a blizzard, biting cold, now the withering oven heat of the desert.

Shredded Novel

The night I arrived in Puerto Vallarta to give singing lessons to Señor Ramón Pradera, formerly chief of police but now a dentist, was a very dark night indeed.

*

First we heaped flowers around and inside the pink pavilion. They turned out to be camellias, so they did nothing to attenuate the foul smell of fish. Yet it was on that beach, with my eyes glued to Laura's diamond-studden anklet, that I heard for the first time the call of the koël bird saluting the dawn. Pradera stood guard while Laura stripped.

*

Our cathedral organist was a crisp young fellow, hatless, on account of the hurricane, but no more than forty.

*

With a dreadful cry the Prince flung those banknotes into the furnace. Would his friend never arrive? A smirk on Pradera's face elevated the points of his moustache.

*

The retablo portrayed the Virgin. Above the child's lips, as we approached, her nipple – it was not flat, it was elevated, a button. The organist was stretching his fingers out to turn the button. 'He has survived his memory attack!' Laura gasped. 'This must be it,' said our organist, 'the button really is less than half the size of a netsuke and carved in the form of a very tiny Coatlicue.'

*

A white rat had wrecked the pelican's nest. It had buried Domingo's stolen harp in the seaweed wall. Domingo put a hand to his mouth, admiring the remnants of seaweed embroidery.

*

There could no longer be any doubt about it: the existence of the bubble changed everything.

*

Once the lamp had been extinguished, Pradera got down to business. I collected the teeth in the velvet bag, but felt a touch of panic. What if symphorines were fluttering in the dank air? Symphorines? As I groped for the teeth, I thought once more of Gerasimov and the elections. Why was Pradera planting his bony knees on my chest?

*

The great blue heron, still absorbed in his silence, was gazing into the water. On and on Laura sang; she hoped her song might become unearthly and induce remorse, perhaps.

From Earth Myriad Robed

1

Why do I hide from this? I see two sides of what I hide from. On one side a sheet of flame. On the other side a violet horn or the horn of a violet (sharper ears might figure which) would have to envelop no secret oil, no quintessence, but a leg of lamb. Then the obstacle flies apart. Out of this horn a pit is made, and the pit exhales a sizzle and three puffs of smoke. But in Madrid a great lady sits, back straight, on her terracotta throne, and she is on both sides. From her, too, I have been hidden. I was hidden from her slow phantom pace through her costumes in history, from the shock of her arrival – from the contraction of her excavated splendour into the clay, this instant. What hid will not be me if only I can touch, without breaking it, a single contour of the uncontainable.

2

Most probably the cook built it with forethought. The scheme haunting his mind might have been Praxitelean, but he fattened that scheme with fierce Turkish caprice. The skeleton sparkled in the depths of his daydreams and a two-pronged plot, just as probably, rose to the forefront of the cook's mind when he balanced his resources against the fortune he might pocket, once his caprice could be made flesh, fully apparent.

The indoors aspect of his restaurant bore on its lintel an inscription in bold Latin capitals: TURKISH KITCHEN DELICATES FIŞIS AND KEBAP. Outside there was dusty space enough for a flock of goats. Here he shook sackfuls of cement into a revolving iron egg. Here he hosed water into the egg for to make a heavy cement paste. With a shovel he turned the cement until it was hardening. Then did he create with it a circular pond to contain water deep enough for fişis therein to outlive the blaze of day. Therefore into the centre of the pond he plunged a pump to circulate the water and to cool it as it flowed. Now he constructed a raised channel with more cement. In the form of a square he constructed it, to frame the dusty space, his kitchen, water chuckling as it flowed anticlockwise along the channel contained by the low walls he clapped into shape with a board. Not otherwise had aforetimes lavish Aegean air circled columns in the peristyle of a temple, to cool the violet interior, where dwelled, ever fresh, in his happiness, at his repose, the god.

Then came the long branches of eucalyptus trees, for the cook did send forth a throng of boys to gather branches from the shore, weathered branches, none thicker than a boy's wrist. And they did gather many; that throng of boys barefoot gathered many and laid them for him in the dust. Now did he trim the branches and he did prop them one against another and he did fix the uppermost twigs and lock them together like the antlers of Hittite stags, and he spaliered the branches on a tilt to support, across a sloped continuous ridge, two long strips of plastic guttering, one above the other, the lower strip concave, the upper strip flat, as a shelf for flasks of orange and lemon juice. Between these gutterings, just above a man's height, he lodged eight empty plastic bottles on their sides, not all of one same capacity, no, but none less than a gallon bottle. He did then perforate each bottle, top and base, so that, once he had coupled the bottles, water soon would flow from one into the next, the first or eighth being the largest and blue, the others being without colour save for their red screw tops. Experimentally then did he let water into the blue bottle and it flowed, through the other seven, at various velocities, none too fast, finally to gush from a spout, made of a shining shoe horn, back into the circular fishpond. Now did he verily set the pump to work and with a great splutter the circuit sprang to life. Water pumped from the pond flowed along the framing channel of low walls and rose by its own motion and pressure into the blue bottle, chugged through the other seven bottles, and dropped back down the shining shoe horn spout into the pond again.

There was also a shade tree set not far back from the blue bottle. To the stout trunk of this tree he did now fasten with clamps of lustrous tin a vertical neon tube, for the shedding of light upon the scene, when twilight should have descended. And he tucked an insulated flex, black and thick, between the tree trunk and the neon tube; all the way back to the roof of the restaurant he then did run the flex in a loop. Out of the flex he teased the wires of fine copper and from these he did hang half a dozen fairy lights, red, yellow, and blue, for now too the electricity could flow, not, he hoped, intermittently, as is its habit thereabouts, but steadily, so that with a certain aurora the fairy lights would sponge the smoke and dust of his arena.

Hard by his cooking pit in the dust he did hang a bell from a spike, and to this bell he tied a cord, the other end of which he fastened somewhere else, so that from almost anywhere in his arena he could pluck the cord and ring the bell. Across the dust, his centre of command, next he did trundle a big tin box with a turning spit in it, and afterward he set beside it with a loud clink, like that of an armoured man bounding into the saddle, an icebox containing a squadron of tincapped beverage bottles. Swigging vigorously from one of these he swung his arms, lifted and stamped his feet, thus and thus; so did he school his waiters not to trip but to skip or pirouette across the walled water channel at his bell's behest. As in a bastion there he now stood, plucking on his cord. Like acrobats the waiters bore aloft to his guests their flashing trays of food and drink, and his guests were ravished to be served nocturnally by such nimble acrobats.

Then did he put on his hat, not stiff and tall like the hat of an hotel cook, but flat and floppy, almost like the hat of a sailor. He took in one hand his long knife and with one stroke severed clean in half a lamb's backside; and anon with his long fierce fork he pronged into my mouth a lamb's testicle, hot from his grill, a gift. He waved his net into the fishpond and pulled a fat fish out, the length of a cubit, a sea trout, and the fish writhed in the net. Its glittering flesh was firm and cold to my touch, and all the while woodsmoke poured from his pit into my nostrils I could taste times out of mind; I saw a web of wrinkles run across the gong-smooth face of a nomad girl and turning into a tiny globe the solo hoot of an Andalusian owl; in a bellshaped, windshook, goatskin tent I lay and heard breath quicken, faster and faster the thump of coupling.

In the second or seventh plastic bottle the cook had housed a young turtle. Gazing far into the night, measuring his mighty words, he did prophesy that when the turtle was grown so big, so big, then would it burst its bottle, then would come the moment, the countertrigonometrical moment, at which every particle he had raised into manifestation would in a flash attain perfection and so melt away, retrieved by the infinite. For then, too, the insulation of the fairy light flex, burned through by the neon's gentle heat, would perish, the shade tree would explode in a sheet of flame and everybody would be electrocuted. Yet for that moment the blaze would everywhere transfigure the night, even far out at sea, so nobody would mind: the glory of the world when it ended would have no end, and if people grieved at all, they would grieve only during that one moment, haply on account of the turtle being boiled to a turn with nobody there to eat it.

3

Rope sole of a razouteur. Dust beaten out of it. A puff of dust beaten out of a rope sole in a small French hotel, old oak beams overhead. In the puff of dust, vestiges of a village dancing floor. A dancing floor in the dust in a land soaked in blood. The features of Elif: mop of tight black curls, dolphin eyebrows, immense dark eyes, small straight nose, her breath from lips parting. Elif in her satin dress, pale golden satin with a blue sash. And the pounding of the music, in the village dust, the puff of dust gone, Elif gone, into the smoke.

The moment of the pigeon when it hovers in the white zenith of a fountain, splashed, uncontainable, the moment of the pigeon. The moment of the wave when it crests. The moment when the wave peaks, mountainous, and orchestrates its prisms to catch the flying light.

The straight back of Elif dancing, all ten years of her, the milling motion of her hands, prints of her bare feet in the dust. A full moon had risen, its globe slowly flew over the distant headland. Smoke from the fire, woodsmoke. The moment of the fat when it spills into embers and the smoke went up, a white flock of smoke, when the smoke is wool, when the owl hoots, when Elif is a lamb, when she mills her hands, as if winding wool with fingers of spindle, wrists arched like ibis beaks.

The throne she sat in was of wood and canvas. She sat in it on the far side of the fire, chin in hand. At a sign she flew across dust between the young men dancing and back again holding in each hand an empty beer bottle. Prints of her bare feet in the dust, erased by the stamping of feet in razouteurs. The throne she sat in was terracotta or maybe stone. She sat with her back straight, wearing a pale gold satin dress, for tonight, the moment when it was tonight, she had not remembered to wear her Ishtar headscarf. And as she flew again across the dust of the dancing floor, she held in each hand a foaming beer bottle.

I had not made any sign to her, but now she stood near. She spoke, at first with a little smile, in surges, at times in leafy whispers, now and then with cries, low but sharp, apparently in a gibberish she was inventing, but always as if it was a great adventure to speak. Some phrases I heard as Greek, others as Turkish. Several sounds I must have misheard, glossing them as English, but her voice drew them up, I thought, while she sang them out, from an origin as indistinct as Hurrian. As she spoke she pointed a finger, this way and that.

> – Tais da efendim (so she said, standing near)
>   bu ghejeh
>   ti theleis ti theleis efendim
>   surleyebilir musunuz yakoondala

> – oosa ana tanta asnula kyriye
>   ishmek ishki inghiliz tek ort poro
>   tek ort poro yabanchuh…ti theleis?

> – aire kai philia
>   aire kai kypris
>   kuruk chok su
>   kuruk adam efendim

- Poompanul
  poompan simi not

- him father fall down rock
  sky him all hurt
  nunca nunca

- ek te homileo
  ek te midolor homileo
  lütfen bu yazar
  midolor yazar midolor insan dolor

- nehden nehden selene
  io nata ikon elithosiniu
  sema athanato sema polychrono
  io nata io nata chabuk oosa
  ana kai roon…ula roon…kai karanlik
  yok palas…tek lokanta poro

Here she ran off across a corner of the dancing floor, vanished into an invisible room behind the canvas throne, and soon she was coming back through the smoke with a bowl of ice and another bottle of raki. She set them silently on the table and for moments she stood and looked, tilting her head, and did not speak, did not move. Then with three fingers forming a little trefoil-like triangle, once and lightly she struck the silver Berber talisman on my chest, and she was whispering again:

- baba
  baba ti linos mi linos…halk müzik
  tok asnula singtok
  singit rhythmon dalul danstokala
  tok thether baba…ti linos…benim müziyim
  thayat awa biles singis binot killet
  binot killet…
  ne akshamleyin ne de sabahleyin

And then her lips closed and she was gazing at the sky. Her throat moved as if she were swallowing, and when she looked at me again she was saying

- dans kuklon
  kuklon dans

- lütfen bu yaz…bu yaz

    – sikilos efter poh...seeyin
      ahas longas yulif...shine

    – shimdi gitmem lazum

And she did have to go, her father called to her; huge faces lit by candle flames change their shapes, people feasting sit at long tables in a semicircle, and she is running among them, carrying plates of lamb and fish and cabrito, keeping the glasses full.

    Stamping of the feet and stretching the arms out, hand on a hip and hand in the air, the click of the fingers has to perpetuate something, a form, a throb from the footsoles touching the dust and rushing a wave up through the midriff into the shoulders, darkening the blood contained by the domes of the fingertips clicking brushed by the ball of the thumb where from the centre printed in skin tissue the spiral branches out, flesh to its limit carries the pulse and the dance measure remembers a labyrinth, even though we dance rough, whooping and hooting, the land is soaked in blood, the circle is broken and we stumble only fractions of it...So that was why these peoples dance in a circle, even two by two inviting memory of a circle – otherwise they might totter singly away, stringing out, lost forever in the distances of Asia, as others are lost in individuality. And there was a tomb far off, brooding vacantly; more near, undiscovered, a seashell had evolved from its node. A bud of rose, a tomb's peaked lid, I remember these, for now the moment of the pigeon makes the twin peaks of Elif's upper lip more than those alone. More now than purely thoughtful she came back, just once, she came back and chose to give me her hands. I would have heaped them with apples, but none grow there. I would have given her a flock of silky black tinkling goats, a box of stories and sketchbooks and pencils, rolls of embroidery, bushels of wheat, her school fees, an orchard I would have given her, a family of ponies in it, but, as it is, I take her suffering with me, and stupidly I tell her "Ya no hay remedio," for a wind in reverse, enormous cyclone, pulls her backwards into the future, pretty soon its teeth will have torn her wings off. Hearing behind her the howl of that wind, Elif has become an outline against a rose trellis, a figure unwinking, mantled, enthroned, in a faraway tomb frieze, and now I'm gone, the dust is nowhere, Elif nowhere, stretching her arms out. The dust, with her long gaze she has fathomed it.

4

The shadow of abstraction lifts from the writing. It is joined soon by the shadow of emotion. The shadows mix, penetrate one another, and obliterate everything, everything except the sound of writing. This is not the clatter of keys, not the yawns of the mouth mouthing words that call to be written. She had told me, Elif had told me, *bu yaz*, write this down. You don't yawn in the face of an Elif; she had said her sorrow is the people's sorrow, *insan dolor*.

As the shadows lift and mix, another phrase is obliterated: .*tek ort poro*. I hear it again and am being told – This place is a limit, a threshold. To the sound of writing I must reduce that limit. The sound is not the scratching of a head, not the creak of a chair, not knees cracking. A dust devil spins over an oblong of flowers which wait to be named. Never heard a dust devil sound like that before. A dust devil spinning over bushy oblongs of flowers waiting to be named.

So the male imagines that he constructs, but finally a negative will, till then secret, pops out. Protective the female stands in the circle of dust, juggling oranges; she cups a hand and fields with it the fierce male shots, to add one orange after another to her circus of oranges. Has Ahab heard the scream of Queequeg dying? Ahab has heard the scream and peglegs below deck to discover, tattooed over Queequeg's body, the map of a whole tribal universe. Suddenly Ahab has discovered this universe in the scream too. He brandishes his whalebone cane, shakes his repaired leg, orders his ship about, the China Seas are soon behind, the distances disappear, and instead of a whale it is oranges for Ahab. He has arrived in Valencia, he will spend the September of his life juggling oranges, more and more of them, standing in a dusty square. While Queequeg, recovered, tosses oranges to Ahab, Ahab juggles them, to re-enact for pleasure the whole tattoo inscribed in Queequeg's skin. It is the sound of writing. The sound of writing is the whizz of the oranges, the swish of flails beating flax, it is the thud of feet which dance for the life of Linos, so she said, so Elif said, on the threshold, and for the bondage of Linos to death, of which she said nothing. So we speak of linen and bond. So we do scratch the air until, out of it, come the shouts of the Great Shining Cook of Dalyan, in response, giving no mercy, to the whisper of a spirit in Patara.

The Turkish Rooftops

Turkish country people like to sleep on rooftops. In bowers made of dry leaves or in nests of reed they can be found sleeping in the night or during the day. Village houses have one ground floor where in rooms framed by divans families gather, having first taken off their shoes, on or around rugs of many colours, as close as possible to their earth. On the flat rooftops they sleep as close as possible to their sky. Inside the house, they take shelter. But their resourcefulness, generally, is epitomized in the way they ply, without fuss, between the interior and the exposed aspects of the house. Upon the Euclidean geometry of the house – a cellular cube with a flat lid – is mounted another, unstable geometry in which volumes of whatever description fold like breaths alternately in and out. For all the clutter to be found on it, the rooftop signifies The Uncontainable – το ᾿Αχωρήτον – as if the purpose of bodies might be to pick away the contradiction, opaque or luminous, of their skin, thus to be unhoused.

Or is it the purpose of bodies to lean so far out that they can read what is inscribed upon their skin? For on almost any country rooftop the bower is ringed, the surface checkered, by variously significant utensils. Turkish country people like to have their tools and the products of their labour arrayed around them, even in sleep. Also laundry hangs there, drying. In pots of earthenware or tin there will be flowers growing: on trumpet vines flowers of startling blue open at first light, close again in the baking heat of noon, open again if ever the onset of night cools the air. The flowers are sprinkled early and later with water from hosepipes that Turkish people flourish at all hours to settle the dust. On the rooftops, too, there is dust. It has to be hosed away, every so often. Every so often, no less, a cat has to be frightened away, with a shout and a stamping foot. Not so the singular immobile objects. What is this assemblage of zinc barrels, two or three, supported by a metal frame? What is this tangle of rods? On a neighbouring rooftop, across the dusty potholed street, can that actually be the driver's cabin of a delivery truck? That curly object on yet another roof is definitely a tuba, for many years unburnished, left behind by a passing army. And even further off, between this rooftop and the distant temple, you can identify the fresher ruins of a sewing machine.

History has swept across the Turkish rooftops all too often. Utensils live their life still uncongealed; certain other objects, not yet dust, are not really débris but relics, relics jettisoned by hordes on horseback, Macedonian footsloggers, Hittite infantry, and a dull glow still envelops them, forgotten though their origin and use may now be. Soon it may even be forgotten that this miniature Byzantine cathedral, with its towers and cupolas, was borne from street to street on the back of a man who for a coin or two dispensed cups of water from it.

A staircase ascends to the rooftop. It is attached to an outside wall. The stairs are of brick, whitewashed, not very wide, often in fact quite narrow, so that if two people were to meet near the top, one going up and the other down, one of those two people would have to flatten himself against the wall and take a deep breath, or the other might topple off the outer edge and crash through the vine trellis that overshadows a small patio below. (Overshadows, but there is more to it: as summer advances, the grapes fatten in their clusters, innumerable silhouettes of leaf, grape, bird or branch of lemon tree engulf the patio and disperse intricate mobile designs across its floor.) In any event, there is no handrail on the outside edge of the staircase. Seldom will you find two Turkish people, either, flattening themselves against the wall or plunging side by side through the trellis. There is a code and the code is observed. Ascent or descent is accomplished without hurry by one Turkish person at a time.

Buckets, parts of cooking stoves, donkey saddles, lengths of rope, piping, sinks, scythes – if you were to survey, on foot or with a telescope, the rooftops of an entire village, you would find a certain constant mass of more or less identical objects, but also a fringe of original and unique objects. The presence of the latter must signify, surely, this or that degree of variance from the norm to which this or that rooftop denizen has risen by dint of enterprise. Not every rooftop has in its repertory of objects a tangle of rods, a paraffin lamp, or a potted oleander. But in very hot villages the bower is a constant. It will be so situated that the least breeze makes the leaves rustle or reeds whisper. Every bower will rustle in the least breeze, so keen is the bower constructor's perception of the sky, so precise the attunement of his imagination to the sky's whims.

The assemblage of barrels mounted on one another in their frame is a water supply. Heated by the sun, the water gushes down (either on the roof or after passing through a pipe into the interior of the house) for a body to be washed; usually the intimacy of the interior is preferred, except by the rudest of travellers who have been welcomed, guests on the rooftop. Nobody can remember what the tangle of rods is, but still it has its place up here, perhaps merely as a ghostly presence to be stepped around. Or else it is a sky trap. When you wake up among the trumpet vines you might find a piece of the sky, nocturnal animal, snared in it, still groaning, shuddering a bit. Perhaps that is what my grandfather found. Why else would he have refused one day to strap his Byzantine water cathedral to his back and the next gone off to Izmir in search of a ship?

Remember how, in Cézanne's paintings of Mont Sainte Victoire, the mountain changes its clothes, sky its diagonals that shine or rain down upon the roof of the mountain. Dense oil or transparent watercolour, the picture itself is this threshold of contact between orders of objects, present as rock, represented in the picturing act as liquid, remember. Well, every bower envelops a low platform made of wood. A thin mattress is laid over the wood. Over the mattress is laid a woven rug, and cushions are placed for the sleeper's head to rest on; perhaps a thin, if not threadbare, blanket will also be there. A thin blanket, brown or gray. A threadbare blanket. Dust billows out when you shake it. A blanket.

Optimally there will be a mosquito net. A delicate white cocoon, folded back by day its flaps are released at night and secured by strings. Probably many Turkish babies have been conceived on rooftops; tired women refresh themselves in these bowers; in their nests old men look up at the moon and recover hope.

On some Turkish rooftops you will see oblongs of concrete from which steel rods stick out, some askew, some perpendicular. The oblongs are positioned symmetrically, but the rods go every which way, and some do say they are an eyesore. Why are they there? Is it to anchor a new storey eventually to be built over the rooftop, so that the enclosure of any one present rooftop will lead to the unfolding of another, higher up, even closer to the sky, even cooler than the one the new storey will have enclosed, and so up and up, like a squared ziggurat? Some say the new storey will never be written, I mean built, but that Turkish people cling so fondly to their idea that nothing can ever be finished, nothing achieved, that they leave the oblongs there, with rods sticking out, to remind them always that life is impermanent, it is improvised, therefore they imagine rather than complete the upward extension, so the oblongs of concrete are ritual supports, not for new rooms but for ancient and compulsive imaginings, the forgotten past has its ruses, mischief in the air, now where was I? Others again say that if an addition is evidently projected but not yet finished you avoid paying tax. Even the last explanation admits a principle. It is a principle pervading many features of life on Turkish rooftops: let every matter lie open, the boiling stuff of existence stays greener if no lid is put on it, earth calls to its lover the sky, sky calls back to earth, the transparency of a few dashes of intense blue or peach in a watercolour mountain may tomorrow condense into an oil colour so richly glowing that the mountain, tutored by the painter, in whose visions at first light, torrential but caught behind closed eyelids and configuring of their own accord, rock was turned into air, is shipped on its way apparently to Mohammad.

From such a rooftop you hear many voices. Night or day, human voices, animal voices. A rooster is crowing. Chickens thoughtfully cluck. A donkey brays. The little owl chants its one and only note, sometimes trilling it. Frogs instruct the stars to relax, relax. Out of nowhere a momentary song has floated into and out of the mouth of a girl in the street below. Or the timber trucks thunder by, the minaret emits a gravelly voice, that of an illtempered old man, Allah Allah, enraged to have been woken up, he is reaching for his sword, Akbar.

Toward nightfall, listen for the drum. An old drum is being thumped among the huts, under the eucalyptus trees, a clarinet has joined it, playing a wiry tune, spiral, to the monotonous beat of the drum it adds a melody, a catch.

Somewhere down there, people are streaming toward the huts, in serious clothes, wizards in peaked caps, young men with fresh haircuts. Always the drumbeat, still the clarinet's catch. With or without your telescope – if with it, then be sure to wipe the oil or watercolour off its lens – you see the drummer, a brown old village man, made of olive wood, and the stick in his fingers never misses a single beat of the three it is capable of. The clarinet player is young, his lungs sepia with nicotine, but he is blowing without let-up, the catch is attractive. Duly the crowd is ushered through a gap in the fence just before the Pepsi sign. People push through, the drummer will drum for them, the clarinetist blow for them long after all have settled in their ring around the dance floor. There, another music, more densely enormous, has now begun, and the wedding feast explodes, women dancing first, soon joined by uncles and fathers, finally by capering young men with arms outspread.

By this time you are with them, but as you spread your own arms look back to your rooftop. Hearing in contradiction the two musics, one dense, one transparent, you now conceive of the rooftop not as their analogue but as yet another threshold, altogether distinct, at which resemblances vanish, vanishing points of brilliant green and cool rose converge on the breathlike peril of substance, the deep ground of their volatility: a platform shrouded by leaves dried ochre by the air.